GOOD

FINDING HEALTHY **BALANCE**

IN

IN A CULTURE OF **EXTREMES**

TENSION

STUDY GUIDE

Copyright © 2024 by Jeremy Yancey

Published by Arrows and Stones

All rights reserved. No portion of this book may be reproduced, stored in a retrieval system, or transmitted in any form or by any means—electronic, mechanical, photocopy, recording, scanning, or other—except for brief quotations in critical reviews or articles, without prior written permission of the author.

Unless otherwise marked, all Scripture quotations are taken from the Holy Bible, New International Version®. Copyright © 1973, 1978, 1984, 2011 by Biblica, Inc.™ Used by permission of Zondervan. All rights reserved worldwide. www.zondervan.com. The "NIV" and "New International Version" are trademarks registered in the United States Patent and Trademark Office by Biblica, Inc.™ | Scripture quotations marked GNT are from the Good News Translation in Today's English Version- Second Edition Copyright © 1992 by American Bible Society. Used by Permission. | Scripture quotations marked NKJV are taken from the New King James Version®. Copyright © 1982 by Thomas Nelson. Used by permission. All rights reserved.

For foreign and subsidiary rights, contact the author.

Cover design by Sara Young
Cover photo by Kellie Gann

ISBN: 978-1-960678-39-3   1 2 3 4 5 6 7 8 9 10

Printed in the United States of America

GOOD

FINDING HEALTHY **BALANCE**

IN

IN A CULTURE OF **EXTREMES**

TENSION

JEREMY YANCEY

STUDY GUIDE

ARROWS &
STONES

CONTENTS

Chapter 1. A Tension Deficit 6

Chapter 2. Flexible Focus 10

Chapter 3. Real Hope 14

Chapter 4. Humbly Confident 18

Chapter 5. Candid And Kind 22

Chapter 6. Running And Resting 26

Chapter 7. Listening and Speaking 30

Chapter 8. In-Tension-al Living 34

Chapter 9. A Prayer That's Taut 38

GOOD

FINDING HEALTHY **BALANCE**

IN

IN A CULTURE OF **EXTREMES**

TENSION

JEREMY YANCEY

CHAPTER 1

A TENSION DEFICIT

HEALTHY TENSION: Jesus wants to help you find it and live in it.

READING TIME

As you read Chapter 1: "A Tension Deficit" in *Good in Tension*, reflect on, and respond to the text by answering the following questions.

REFLECT AND TAKE ACTION:

When have you experienced tension recently?

_____
_____
_____
_____
_____
_____
_____

What was the tension surrounding? How did it make you feel?

_____
_____
_____
_____
_____
_____
_____

Do you avoid tension? Why or why not?

_____
_____
_____
_____
_____
_____
_____

> *Be wise as serpents and harmless as doves.*
>
> —Matthew 10:16 (NKJV)

Consider the scripture above and answer the following questions:

What is the meaning of this passage?

_____
_____
_____
_____

What tension is present between the two states mentioned in the verse?

_____
_____
_____
_____
_____

What is the difference between vacillation and oscillation? Which should we strive for?

_____
_____
_____
_____
_____

How would you define "healthy tension"?

What are "extremes"? When have you been guilty of going to them?

What is currently holding you back from healthy tension?

CHAPTER 2

FLEXIBLE FOCUS

Flexibility with focus. Grace and truth in harmony.

READING TIME

As you read Chapter 2: "Flexible Focus" in *Good in Tension*, reflect on, and respond to the text by answering the following questions.

REFLECT AND TAKE ACTION:

Why did Peter lose the ability to walk on the water?

_____
_____
_____
_____
_____
_____
_____

What do you focus on in life?

_____
_____
_____
_____
_____
_____
_____

How do you stay focused on what truly matters?

_____
_____
_____
_____
_____
_____
_____

> *Let us keep our eyes fixed on Jesus, on whom our faith depends from beginning to end.*
>
> —Hebrews 12:2 (GNT)

Consider the scripture above and answer the following questions:

What stands out to you from this verse?

_____
_____
_____
_____
_____

What does this passage mean when it states our faith "depends" on Jesus?

_____
_____
_____
_____
_____

Have you ever let distractions take your focus off Jesus? What was the distraction?

_____
_____
_____
_____
_____

How did you overcome the distraction?

In what other areas of your life do you need to minimize distractions?

Why is rigidity dangerous?

Is extreme flexibility good? Why or why not?

CHAPTER 3

REAL HOPE

Yes, we will go through difficult times when our hopes are faint, but we put our hope in a powerful God. That's the reality we live in.

READING TIME

As you read Chapter 3: "Real Hope" in *Good in Tension*, reflect on, and respond to the text by answering the following questions.

REFLECT AND TAKE ACTION:

Why did Caleb and Joshua's report differ from the rest of the spies?

_____
_____
_____
_____
_____
_____
_____

Have you ever hoped for something only to be let down by reality? What was it?

_____
_____
_____
_____
_____
_____
_____

What are you hoping for? Is this realistic?

_____
_____
_____
_____
_____
_____
_____

> *"Suppose a king is about to go to war against another king. Won't he first sit down and consider whether he is able with ten thousand men to oppose the one coming against him with twenty thousand?"*
>
> —Luke 14:31

Consider the scripture above and answer the following questions:

What does this verse reveal about setting expectations?

___
___
___
___
___

How does this verse apply to your current hopes, dreams, or vision?

___
___
___
___
___

Are you more hopeful or more realistic?

___
___
___
___
___

How can you continue to be hopeful while also staying realistic?

___

Do you think you have ever been delusional in your goal-setting or what you hope for? Have you ever witnessed this in someone else?

___

Have you ever struggled with pessimism? Surrounding what?

___

What do you put your hope in? Is it something or someone other than God?

___

CHAPTER 4

HUMBLY CONFIDENT

Insecurity can become either quicksand or jet fuel.

READING TIME

As you read Chapter 4: "Humbly Confident" in *Good in Tension*, reflect on, and respond to the text by answering the following questions.

REFLECT AND TAKE ACTION:

What are you insecure about or have you been insecure about in the past?

_____
_____
_____
_____
_____
_____

What formed this insecurity?

_____
_____
_____
_____
_____
_____
_____

How would you define being confident in your own words? How does this differ from arrogance?

_____
_____
_____
_____
_____
_____
_____

> *Pride goes before destruction, a haughty spirit before a fall.*
> —Proverbs 16:18

Consider the scripture above and answer the following questions:

What is a "haughty spirit"?

_____
_____
_____
_____
_____

What can you do to defend against a mindset of pride and a haughty spirit?

_____
_____
_____
_____
_____

What are you confident in?

_____
_____
_____
_____
_____

Would you consider yourself to be humble? Why or why not?

How do you differentiate between shame and humility?

How did David demonstrate confident humility?

CHAPTER 5

CANDID AND KIND

True kindness—God's kind of love—rejoices in the truth and expresses that truth as needed.

READING TIME

As you read Chapter 5: "Candid And Kind" in *Good in Tension*, reflect on, and respond to the text by answering the following questions.

REFLECT AND TAKE ACTION:

Why is it so important to speak the truth in love?

_____
_____
_____
_____

What happens when we speak the truth without love?

_____
_____
_____
_____

What occurs when we put our love for others above the truth?

_____
_____
_____
_____

Have you ever struggled to speak the truth in love? When? About what?

_____
_____
_____
_____
_____
_____

> *Be completely humble and gentle; be patient, bearing with one another in love. Make every effort to keep the unity of the Spirit through the bond of peace.*
>
> —Ephesians 4:2-3

Consider the scripture above and answer the following questions:

What is the meaning of this passage?

_____
_____
_____
_____
_____
_____

What does it mean to "bear with one another in love"?

_____
_____
_____
_____
_____
_____

Has anyone ever been overly critical of you? How did it make you feel?

_____
_____
_____

Do you know any "flatterers"? Have you ever been guilty of omitting the truth to appear kind?

In what ways is kindness powerful?

CHAPTER 6

RUNNING AND RESTING

*Throughout Jesus's ministry, He seemed
to follow a divine timetable.*

READING TIME

As you read Chapter 6: "Running And Resting" in *Good in Tension*, reflect on, and respond to the text by answering the following questions.

REFLECT AND TAKE ACTION:

Summarize the situation with Lazarus. Why did Jesus wait to go to him?

_____
_____
_____
_____
_____
_____

Have you ever struggled to know the correct timing of big decisions in your life? If so, which decisions?

_____
_____
_____
_____
_____
_____

How often do you go to God for guidance in this area?

_____
_____
_____
_____
_____
_____

> *Let us run with perseverance the race marked out for us.*
>
> —Hebrews 12:1

Consider the scripture above and answer the following questions:

What kind of race is this scripture referring to?

_____
_____
_____
_____

What do you think it looks like to "run with perseverance"?

_____
_____
_____
_____

Do you have a harder time running or resting? Which do you need to do more of?

_____
_____
_____
_____
_____
_____

Is resting really necessary? What will occur when we don't get rest?

How do you ensure you don't become frantic but also that you don't become complacent?

Are you running entirely on your own energy, or are you leaning on God?

CHAPTER 7

LISTENING AND SPEAKING

*Speech is not just for transmitting information.
It's for building relationships.*

READING TIME

As you read Chapter 7: "Listening and Speaking" in *Good in Tension*, reflect on, and respond to the text by answering the following questions.

REFLECT AND TAKE ACTION:

In what ways is communication a two-way street?

_____
_____
_____
_____
_____
_____
_____
_____
_____

When talking with someone, do you tend to speak more or listen more? Explain.

_____
_____
_____
_____
_____
_____
_____
_____
_____
_____
_____
_____
_____

> *Those who consider themselves religious and yet do not keep a tight rein on their tongues deceive themselves, and their religion is worthless.*
>
> —James 1:26

Consider the scripture above and answer the following questions:

What is the meaning of this passage?

___

How do these "religious people" deceive themselves?

___

What is "active listening"? How can you practice this?

___

Have you or someone you know ever dominated a conversation? What was the result?

Where is the line between closely listening to someone and seeming withdrawn from the conversation altogether?

What area of your conversation do you feel you most need to work on?

CHAPTER 8

IN-TENSION-AL LIVING

The Bible is not just a bunch of pious thoughts for some ethereal plane of existence. No, it's cutting-edge wisdom for the grit and grime of each day.

READING TIME

As you read Chapter 8: "In-Tension-al Living" in *Good in Tension*, reflect on, and respond to the text by answering the following questions.

REFLECT AND TAKE ACTION:

How often do you study God's Word? When do you read?

_____
_____
_____
_____
_____
_____

If you are married, do you and your spouse communicate both candidly and kindly? How can you personally balance these traits better?

_____
_____
_____
_____
_____
_____

How can you be more focused yet flexible in your parenting? Which of these two areas do you need to work on?

_____
_____
_____
_____
_____
_____

> *Everyone should be quick to listen, slow to speak and slow to become angry.*
>
> —James 1:19

Consider the scripture above and answer the following questions:

Is there any area of your life where you are not quick to listen? Family life? Politics?

_____
_____
_____
_____
_____
_____

When was the last time someone else made you angry? How did they anger you?

_____
_____
_____
_____
_____
_____

What gifts do you possess that can benefit the church? How can you utilize these gifts to serve with confidence and humility?

_____
_____
_____
_____

Do you have a balance of running and resting in your spiritual life? How can you better balance these?

Of the six tensions listed, which do you feel you are the most unbalanced within? Explain your answer.

Are you attempting to balance these tensions with your own strength and wisdom, or are you relying on God's assistance?

CHAPTER 9

A PRAYER THAT'S TAUT

*Phrase by phrase, the Lord's prayer tunes us.
The healthy tensions of our lives are examined
and counterbalanced with every line.*

READING TIME

As you read Chapter 9: "A Prayer That's Taut" in *Good in Tension*, reflect on, and respond to the text by answering the following questions.

REFLECT AND TAKE ACTION:

In this manner, therefore, pray: Our Father in heaven, Hallowed by Your name. Your kingdom come. Your will be done on earth as it is in heaven. Give us this day our daily bread. And forgive us our debts, as we forgive our debtors. And do not lead us into temptation, but deliver us from the evil one. For Yours is the kingdom and the power and the glory forever. Amen.

—Matthew 6:9-13 (NKJV)

Consider the scripture above and answer the following questions:

What is the significance of Jesus saying, "Our Father"?

_____
_____
_____
_____
_____
_____
_____
_____
_____

In your own words, what does it mean when Jesus said, "Hallowed be thy name"?

_____
_____

What two "homes" do we as Christians live in tension between? Should we focus on one above the other?

Why did Jesus pray for God's will to be done? Is this necessary for it to come to fruition?

What is our "daily bread"?

Which line(s) highlight the forgiveness God wants us to demonstrate to others? Explain

In what ways does God "deliver us" from the evil one?

Take time to meditate on this passage and pray the Lord's prayer.

www.ingramcontent.com/pod-product-compliance
Lightning Source LLC
Chambersburg PA
CBHW070654100426
42734CB00048B/2988